THE BLOOMSBURY GROUP

Frances Spalding

NPG

Published in Great Britain by the National Portrait Gallery Publications,
National Portrait Gallery, St Martin's Place, London WC2H 0HE

ISBN 1 85514 202 3

A catalogue record for this book is available from the British Library

Series Project Editors: Gillian Forrester and Lucy Clark
Series Picture Researcher: Susie Foster
Series Designer: Karen Osborne
Printed by Clifford Press Ltd, Coventry

Front cover
Vanessa Bell, 1879–1961
Duncan Grant, *c.*1918 (detail)
Oil on canvas, 94 x 60.6 cm
© National Portrait Gallery (4331)

For a complete catalogue of current publications,
please write to the address above.

CONTENTS

❦

INTRODUCTION

❧

Bloomsbury portraits are something of an anomaly. To succeed, a portrait is, to some extent, dependent on likeness; yet the artists in this group rejected mimetic veracity in favour of more expressive design and colour. They were inspired partly by Matisse. 'A work of art', wrote Matisse in 1908, in his famous *Notes d'un peintre*, 'must carry in itself its complete significance and impose it on the beholder even before he can identify the subject-matter.' Similarly, Roger Fry, Bloomsbury's chief spokesman on aesthetics, declared in 1913 that artists should 'give up the idea of imitative likeness and aim at the creation of absolutely necessitated form'. Ironically, such views seem to have had little effect on Fry's own portraiture, and in his portraits of Clive Bell and Bertrand Russell 'likeness' plays a surprisingly dominant part. Other Bloomsbury artists found different ways of balancing the needs of a portrait against the picture's formal requirements. What was essential, Fry once said, was 'imaginative characterisation'. This ingredient is variously found in the National Portrait Gallery's Bloomsbury portraits.

The earliest portraits either by or of figures within Bloomsbury predate the excitement caused by Post-Impressionism and owe more to Whistler than Matisse. One of Whistler's legacies to British art had been a sharpened sense of tonal harmony. His example lies behind Vanessa Bell's portrait of Saxon Sydney-Turner, a largely silent member of Bloomsbury who buried his talents in the Treasury. The picture is primarily a study in tone, for the whites in his collar, the sheet music and keyboard deliberately offset the surrounding browns, greys and blacks. Whistler had also done much to popularise certain poses: his memorable portraits of his mother and of Thomas Carlyle made fashionable for a period the seated, profile pose that Duncan Grant employed in his portrait of Cecil Taylor, a Cambridge undergraduate who found his niche teaching Classics at Clifton College, Bristol. Whistler had also favoured the full-length standing portrait that gives dignity to Roger Fry's low-toned portrait of the visionary reformer Edward Carpenter.

Ironically, in 1894, at the time that this portrait was painted, Fry distrusted much modern art. He looked at the work of his fellow colleagues in the New English Art Club and found it wanting. 'I came to feel more and more the absence in their work of structural design,' he later recollected. In reaction against vapid naturalism, he turned his attention to the Old Masters, became a leading art critic, a scholar of Italian art, a friend of Bernard Berenson and the author of the first monograph in English on Giovanni Bellini. In his spare time he continued to paint pictures that looked back to Claude Lorrain in their aspiration towards classical harmony and design. The critic D.S. MacColl pigeon-holed Fry at this time as a 'pastichist of ancients and opponent of modern French painting'.

Much was to happen before Fry underwent a conversion and became, in the eyes of many, the apologist for, and impresario of, modern art. He was busily working as an art critic for the *Burlington Magazine*, which he helped to found, and the Metropolitan Museum of Art in New York during those years when 'Bloomsbury' first came into existence. It started when a group of like-minded individuals began meeting regularly in Bloomsbury, an area of London centred around the British Museum. At

CECIL TAYLOR, Duncan Grant, 1909

JULIA STEPHEN, Julia Margaret Cameron, 1867

the turn of the century it was a respectable, if unfashionable place to live. The Georgian and Victorian houses that surround its squares, with their leafy gardens, are dignified and spacious. The group of friends, who became known by the name given to this area, gathered at 46 Gordon Square, a house taken by Vanessa Stephen in 1904 for herself, her sister Virginia, and her two brothers Thoby and Adrian.

The cause of their move was the death of their twice-widowed father, Leslie Stephen. They left behind a house in Kensington, made dark by its mid-Victorian style of decoration and gloomy by the memory of the deaths of their mother and of their half-sister, Stella Duckworth. 46 Gordon Square represented a new beginning, and to emphasise this fact Vanessa Stephen banished clutter, painted several rooms white and hung in the hallway photographs of famous Victorians opposite a whole row of Julia Margaret Cameron's photographs of their mother, Julia Stephen.

Here, too, Vanessa's brother Thoby began to hold regular 'At Homes'. At first these comprised an awkward mix of old friends and new, but gradually the aunts and family friends stayed away and an inner core emerged, composed chiefly of Thoby's Cambridge friends, who, inspired by the empiricist philosophy of G.E. Moore, discussed, among other things, the concept of 'the good' and the importance of aesthetic experience and personal relations. For Vanessa and Virginia, these 'At Homes' gave them the opportunity to experience the kind of easy ragging and truly exploratory discussion that had been denied them by Leslie Stephen's decision to educate them at home.

This group of friends grew closer during the winter of 1906–7, after Thoby's untimely death from typhoid following a trip to Greece. Another significant development was the marriage in 1907 between Vanessa Stephen and Thoby's friend Clive Bell, whose love of conversation made him a linchpin within Bloomsbury.

Although Clive Bell came from a hunting and shooting background, he had a lively interest in art, which had been developed by a period in Paris after he came down from Cambridge. He had gone to France with the intention of doing historical research, but had spent much of his time in the company of painters. On meeting Roger Fry for the first time in January 1910, he instantly fell into a conversation with him about the need to show modern French art in London.

Now that Cézanne, Van Gogh, Gauguin and Matisse enjoy widespread popularity and high acclaim, it requires an effort of the imagination to appreciate how crude, unfinished and unreal their paintings seemed to the British in 1910. But Roger Fry's 'Manet and the Post-Impressionists' exhibition, held at the Grafton Galleries in London that year, successfully awoke Britain to modern art. Almost overnight, young artists such as Duncan Grant abandoned hard-won skills in favour of a more experimental manner. By the time Fry came to mount his second Post-Impressionist exhibition, in the winter of 1912–13, he was able to include a British selection and to argue in the catalogue: 'Now, these artists do not seek to give what can, after all, be but a pale reflex of actual appearance, but to arouse the conviction of a new and definite reality. They do not seek to imitate form, but to create form; not to imitate life, but to find an equivalent to life.'

Fry's promotion of Post-Impressionism was partly a reaction against the sentimental anecdotalism in British art. Likewise, the Bloomsbury group were in revolt against unthinking acceptance of outdated conventions and moral precepts. In their determination to replace hypocrisy and cant with a free, rational, civilised society, dedicated to the pursuit of truth and beauty, they succeeded in making a definite contribution to the development of liberal thought.

Three of the group's members – Leonard Woolf (who married Virginia Stephen), Lytton Strachey and Saxon Sydney-Turner – had, at Cambridge, developed a passion for the convoluted novels of Henry James. His delicate analysis of motive had encouraged them to adopt what they called 'the method'. This, Leonard Woolf explained, was 'a kind of third-degree psychological investigation applied to the souls of one's friends … a kind of compulsory psychoanalysis'. It became a characteristic of Bloomsbury, who never tired of analysing their own and others' behaviour. This testing habit of mind made them very alert, critical of themselves and others.

SAXON SYDNEY-TURNER, Vanessa Bell, 1908

In their attempt to see things afresh, Bloomsbury cast aside the shibboleths of their elders and tried to accept no standard which did not meet with the approval of their own unaided judgement. A similar willingness to investigate and experiment characterises Bloomsbury art. Soon after Vanessa Bell had adopted a Post-Impressionist manner, she painted three portraits of her sister. In two of these, although the shape of the face is present, the features are omitted or merely suggested, yet a vivid sense of presence is created through the handling of pose, succinct drawing and strong colour oppositions. If these Post-Impressionist portraits are placed alongside portraits by the fashionable painters of the day – Sir Frank Dicksee, Sir John Lavery or John Singer Sargent, for example – they appear radical in their directness and unfussy simplicity.

Vanessa Bell's close relationships with Roger Fry and Duncan Grant fertilised her interests and, like Fry and Grant, she experimented briefly with non-figurative art around 1914. But despite their strong leaning

VIRGINIA WOOLF, Vanessa Bell, 1911–12

SIR FRANK SWETTENHAM
John Singer Sargent, 1904

towards formalism, Bloomsbury artists remained fascinated with the problems set by representation, and portraits, though rarely painted on a commissioned basis, continued to form an important part of their *œuvre*.

The circumstances in which most Bloomsbury portraits were painted were extremely casual. Duncan Grant's oil portrait of Virginia Woolf (Metropolitan Museum of Art, New York) was completely unplanned: it was painted on the spur of the moment while she sat and talked with her sister in a room at 46 Gordon Square, where Grant had his painting things already laid out. Other members of the group found themselves persuaded to sit while on visits to Asheham or Charleston, the Sussex houses that became outposts of Bloomsbury. A more careful pursuit of likeness can be found in Dora Carrington's portraits, in, for example, her memorable

portraits of Lytton Strachey and Gerald Brenan. Carrington stood a little apart from the other Bloomsbury artists, for her work combines close attention to appearances with poetic feeling and has more affinity with the Pre-Raphaelites than the French Post-Impressionists.

The familiarity with each other which these friends enjoyed gives an additional fascination to those Bloomsbury portraits done by members of the inner circle. Just as Virginia Woolf, inspired by the example of painters, argued that fiction needs the 'close touch of life' as well as the distance that 'the gift of style, arrangement, construction' achieves, so portraiture depends on a mixture of aesthetic and non-aesthetic demands. In some instances, as when Vanessa Bell painted a group portrait of a Bloomsbury Memoir Club meeting, the result is less good as a picture than as a record of a unique gathering of minds. But for the most part Bloomsbury portraits construct a memorable interpretation of likeness and character.

Select Bibliography

Isabelle Anscombe, *Omega and After*, Thames and Hudson, 1981.

Clive Bell, *Old Friends*, Chatto and Windus, 1956.

Quentin Bell, *Bloomsbury*, Weidenfeld and Nicolson, 1968.

Quentin Bell, *Virginia Woolf: A Biography*, Vols. I and II, Hogarth Press, 1972.

Anne Oliver Bell (ed.), *The Diary of Virginia Woolf*, Vols. I–V, Hogarth Press, 1977–84.

Hugh and Mirabel Cecil, *Clever Hearts: Desmond and Molly MacCarthy, A Biography*, Victor Gollancz, 1990.

Judith Collins, *The Omega Workshops*, Secker and Warburg, 1983.

Roger Fry, *Vision and Design*, Chatto and Windus, 1920.

P.N. Furbank, *E.M. Forster: A Life*, Vols. I and II, Secker and Warburg, 1977.

Angelica Garnett, *Deceived with Kindness*, Hogarth Press, 1984.

Jane Hill, *The Art of Dora Carrington*, Herbert Press, 1994.

Michael Holroyd, *Lytton Strachey*, Chatto and Windus, 1995.

Hermione Lee, *Virginia Woolf*, Chatto and Windus, 1996.

Paul Levy, *Moore: G.E. Moore and the Cambridge Apostles*, Weidenfeld and Nicolson, 1979.

Nigel Nicolson and J.T. Banks (eds.), *The Letters of Virginia Woolf*, Vols. I–VI, Hogarth Press, 1975–80.

Frances Partridge, *Memories*, Victor Gollancz, 1981.

S.P. Rosenbaum, *Victorian Bloomsbury: The Early Literary History of the Bloomsbury Group*, Vol. I, Macmillan, 1987.

S.P. Rosenbaum, *Edwardian Bloomsbury: The Early Literary History of the Bloomsbury Group*, Vol. II, Macmillan, 1994.

Miranda Seymour, *Ottoline Morrell: Life On the Grand Scale*, Hodder and Stoughton, 1992.

Richard Shone, *Bloomsbury Portraits*, Phaidon Press, 1994.

Frances Spalding, *Roger Fry: Art and Life*, Elek/Granada, 1980.

Frances Spalding, *Vanessa Bell*, Weidenfeld and Nicolson, 1983.

Frances Spalding, *Duncan Grant*, Chatto and Windus, 1997.

Simon Watney, *English Post-Impressionism*, Studio Vista, 1980.

Simon Watney, *The Art of Duncan Grant*, John Murray, 1990.

Leonard Woolf, *Beginning Again: An Autobiography of the Years 1911–1918*, Hogarth Press, 1967.

Leonard Woolf, *Downhill All the Way: An Autobiography of the Years 1919–1939*, Hogarth Press, 1967.

DESMOND MACCARTHY (1877-1952)

❧

'Where they seem to me to triumph,' Virginia Woolf once wrote of her Bloomsbury friends, 'is in having worked out a view of life which was not by any means corrupt or sinister or merely intellectual; rather ascetic and austere indeed; which still holds, and keeps them dining together, and staying together, after 20 years; and no amount of quarrelling or success, or failure has altered this. Now I do think this rather credible.'

One person Virginia Woolf had in mind when she wrote this was Desmond MacCarthy, for his metier was conversation and he remained a vital ingredient within Bloomsbury gatherings. 'Desmond burbling general goodwill and human love', Virginia Woolf wrote in her diary after one dinner at the home of St John and Mary Hutchinson. MacCarthy had by then become one of the most influential literary critics in England, reigning throughout the 1930s and 1940s in the pages of the *Sunday Times*. Virginia Woolf clearly felt that this need to gut a book, to make a synoptic summary in a light, intelligent, amusing way, had by 1934 begun to affect his conversation, for she wrote: 'Talk of [Coventry] Patmore. Desmond expatiated, praised, placed him with Crashaw: described his great love of fires, his son Epiphany, all in the *Sunday Times* agreeable manner, not very close to the object: a love of little pictures.'

Desmond MacCarthy was linked to other members of Bloomsbury through his Cambridge background and through marriage, for his wife, Molly Warre-Cornish, was related to the Stephen family through her aunt by marriage, Lady Ritchie, the novelist Anny Thackeray. Though MacCarthy had begun to make a reputation for himself as a literary and dramatic critic soon after he came down from Cambridge, he and his wife were always short of money. When he was about to become the father of a third child, he was invited by Roger Fry to act as secretary for the first Post-Impressionist exhibition. Notoriously unbusinesslike, he accepted the post and learnt at his interview with the Grafton Gallery that he would receive a share in the profits. This was told him with a pitying smile, as the exhibition was predicted to be a financial failure. To everyone's surprise, MacCarthy walked away with £460 – a lump sum larger than any other he ever earned.

Desmond MacCarthy, Duncan Grant, c.1942

DESMOND MACCARTHY, Duncan Grant, 1944

Duncan Grant painted this portrait of Desmond MacCarthy, and the study for it, at Charleston during the Second World War. Contained by the outline of the chair and cut off from the spectator by the act of reading, the sitter is presented as an affable, reserved individual, dedicated to the life of the mind. MacCarthy once wrote to his mother explaining his disinclination to confide: 'Your confidence! Your confidence! How many men and women are crying for that; husbands to wives, mothers to children; every friend to friend. But there is much included in that word confidence that is better hidden, covered up, is better trampled down. The spirit of dignified selection, what we call reserve, alone makes companionship, yes love, possible. There are spiritual indelicacies just as there are physical indelicacies.'

Virginia Woolf (1882–1941)

❧

'Words are an impure medium,' Virginia Woolf once wrote, 'better far to have been born into the silent kingdom of paint.' In this particular essay she had the painter Walter Sickert in mind, but behind this remark lay a long familiarity with painters. Virginia Woolf lived in a milieu in which paintings and painted decorations were an accepted ingredient in interior designs, and in which exhibitions were often visited, discussed, and reviewed. She was familiar with the smell and clutter of an artist's studio, and she could not pick up one of her own books, with their dustjackets designed by her sister, Vanessa Bell, without having the example of the visual arts constantly before her eyes.

'I shall reform the novel,' she had announced, as early as 1908. Though she did not achieve this aim for many years to come, she was in the meantime to witness the revolution caused by the French Post-Impressionist paintings shown at Roger Fry's two exhibitions. After the second, in 1913, Virginia Woolf expressed mock relief to a friend: 'The Grafton, thank God, is over; artists are an abominable race. The furious excitement of these people all the winter over their pieces of canvas coloured green and blue, is odious.'

Nevertheless, Virginia Woolf not only listened to the theoretical explanation for Post-Impressionism that Roger Fry presented at that time but also sat for her portrait, on more than one occasion, to her sister, who had adopted a Post-Impressionist style. One of these portraits, painted in 1912, is that in the National Portrait Gallery collection. Vanessa Bell portrays her sister leaning back in an armchair, crocheting. Much that is characteristic of the sitter is caught in this broadly treated picture, with its strong, clear, warm–cool colour oppositions and its deliberate avoidance of any detail that might break or disturb the contemplative mood created by the picture's breadth and flow. Even the facial features are suggested rather than defined. Compared with the accepted styles of portraiture that were current at that time, Vanessa Bell's painting is remarkably open and fresh.

With so much evidence around her of a modernist approach to painting, Virginia Woolf began to rethink her attitude to writing. Looking back on this period, she later wrote: 'Literature was suffering from a plethora of old clothes. Cézanne and Picasso had shown the way; writers

Virginia Woolf
Vanessa Bell, 1912

Virginia Woolf
Stephen Tomlin, *c.*1935

should fling representation to the winds and follow suit.' Gradually she did just this. In her novels, she demolished accepted conventions concerning plot and character and replaced them with a roving consciousness capable of dealing with the myriad impressions that chase through the mind on any one day. This 'stream of consciousness' technique characterised her novels, such as *Mrs Dalloway*, *To the Lighthouse* and *Orlando*, the

19

latter celebrating her affair with the novelist Vita Sackville-West. By 1934 she was willing to admit: 'Paintings and writing have much to tell each other, they have much in common.'

Despite her interest in art, Virginia Woolf sat very unwillingly to artists other than her sister. Though Duncan Grant succeeded in catching her likeness (Metropolitan Museum of Art, New York) while she sat talking to her sister, the only artist she actually posed for was Stephen Tomlin, a sculptor who was known to several of her Bloomsbury friends. She also distrusted photographers and, though persuaded to sit for Man Ray in 1934, she refused Cecil Beaton's request to photograph her. A similarly nonchalant attitude to posterity appears in her regard for her letters. She must have known that they might one day be published, yet she wrote at speed, chasing the moment and subtle nuances of experience. When the composer Dame Ethel Smyth wanted to incorporate some of their correspondence into her voluminous autobiography, Virginia Woolf advised: 'Let's leave the letters till we're both dead. That's my plan. I don't keep or destroy but collect miscellaneous bundles of odds and ends, and let posterity, if there is one, burn or not. Let's forget all about death and all about posterity.'

Posterity has made her image by the photographer George Beresford one of the National Portrait Gallery's best-selling postcards. Between 1990 and 1994, the Gallery sold 21,000 cards of this image. Woolf was finally displaced as the number-one hit in the postcard-selling parade by the film star Daniel Day-Lewis.

VIRGINIA WOOLF
George Charles Beresford, 1902

LEONARD WOOLF (1880–1969)

❧

'Leonard is the only person I have ever seen whom I can imagine as the right husband for you.' So Vanessa Bell wrote to her sister, Virginia Stephen, in January 1912. The same thought struck Leonard Woolf's friend Lytton Strachey, two days after he himself had proposed to Virginia and instantly recognised his mistake. At that date Woolf was in Ceylon and had met the Stephen sisters only twice, very briefly. Nevertheless, Strachey wrote: 'I think there's no doubt whatever that you ought to marry her. You *would* be great enough, and you'd have the advantage of physical desire. I was in terror lest she should kiss me.'

In keeping with Strachey's wishes, Leonard Woolf proposed to Virginia Stephen on 11 January 1912. Four months later she accepted him. 'How am I to begin about Leonard?' she wrote to her friend Madge Vaughan.

> *First he is a Jew; second he is 31; third, he spent 7 years in Ceylon, governing natives, inventing ploughs, shooting tigers, and did so well that they offered him a very high place the other day, which he refused, wishing to marry me, and gave up his entire career there on the chance that I would agree. He has no money of his own ... He interests me immensely, besides all the rest. We mean to marry in August, and he wants to find out about labour and factories and to keep outside Government and do things on his own account. He has also written a novel* [The Village in the Jungle, *published 1913*], *and means to write as well as be practical.*
>
> (Nigel Nicolson and J.T. Banks (eds.), The Flight of the Mind: The Letters of Virginia Woolf, Vol. 1: 1888–1912, 1975, p.503)

This character sketch matches the man Leonard Woolf eventually became. Having turned down high office in the colonial civil service, he became an early and persistent advocate for the dismantling of the colonial system. He set up the Hogarth Press, became the publisher of Freud, T.S. Eliot and many others and never published a book purely for commercial reasons. As an adviser to the Labour Party and the Fabian Society he remained a leading proponent of democratic socialism. He was also the author of one of the earliest blueprints for the League of Nations and devoted much of his life to advocating ways of deterring international aggression. In addition, he encouraged and supported through bouts of

LEONARD WOOLF, Vanessa Bell, 1940

mental illness a wife who was one of the literary geniuses of the twentieth century. He was also adept at the many tasks necessary to maintain a garden and had an innate feeling for animals.

In her 1940 portrait of Leonard Woolf, Vanessa Bell caught something of his austere integrity, his homeliness and absorption in his work. A useful *repoussoir* motif is provided by his sleeping spaniel.

VANESSA BELL (1879–1961)

❧

Vanessa Bell was the daughter of the eminent literary historian and critic Sir Leslie Stephen and his second wife, Julia Duckworth (née Jackson). There were four children born of this marriage, and Vanessa was the eldest. It was she who, towards the end of her widowed father's life, had to manage the household and act as hostess to his tea-time guests. The frustrations attendant on these responsibilities and the pressure for her to enter 'society' left her feeling 'vaguely thwarted and repressed and perhaps tantalized sometimes, by glimpses of a life where one might have been at ease'. As a result Vanessa was determined to achieve a freer, less conventional and more honest way of existence after the death of her father in 1904.

She instigated a move to 46 Gordon Square, Bloomsbury, and there the Stephen siblings began holding 'At Homes'. Out of these emerged that inner core of friends to whom the name 'Bloomsbury' became attached. Many who came were Cambridge friends of Thoby Stephen, and they brought with them a respect for the philosophy of G.E. Moore and a love of investigative, ironic and often irreverent talk. One person whose ebullience enlivened these conversations was Clive Bell. When he proposed to Vanessa, she at first refused him, but after Thoby's death from typhoid in 1906, Clive proposed again and this time Vanessa agreed to become his wife.

Although the couple had two sons, Julian and Quentin, their marital relationship soon ended. There was, however, no divorce and no sharp or sudden break in their association, merely a gradual shift into a new relationship, characterised by respectful affection. After a brief affair with Roger Fry, who had a crucial effect on her art, Vanessa established a lasting creative union with Duncan Grant.

Both portraits of Vanessa Bell in the National Portrait Gallery are by Duncan Grant. The first, a half-length seated portrait of around 1915, is one of a handful of pictures that Grant painted of her in which she wears a red evening dress. Its rich colour proved sympathetic to him at a time at which he was deliberately working in a Post-Impressionist style. An even greater gaiety of colour animates his second portrait, painted a couple of years later, at Charleston. In both pictures he managed to suggest changes

VANESSA BELL
Duncan Grant, c.1915

of light and shade chiefly through alterations of hue rather than tone, creating, particularly in the later work, an effect of colouristic brilliance.

By subjecting Vanessa Bell to this treatment, Grant was in effect acknowledging one of the interests they shared and which helped bond their relationship. At a time when bright, strong colour was generally found only in fairgrounds, circus decoration, gypsy caravans and children's toys, its presence in dress or interior decoration transgressed accepted taste. But as early as 1911, after inspecting some Adam rooms in Fitzroy Square, Vanessa had announced, 'I believe elegance is becoming rather tiresome', and in protest had taken herself off to Debenham's to buy green and red stockings. Just how shocking this was can be inferred from a sales assistant's remark at Liberty's in 1914, when someone from the Omega Workshops tried to buy emerald-green silk: 'Emerald, Madam, is a colour we *never* stock.'

Encouraged by Roger Fry's promotion of French Post-Impressionism, Vanessa Bell began to experiment with bold reductionism in her own painting. She produced her most radical work in the years leading up to and during the First World War. Later, after she had returned to more traditional methods of representation, she was admired as a colourist, producing work of great richness and subtlety.

Vanessa Bell's life was hit by tragedy in 1937 when her elder son was killed in the Spanish Civil War. After this she could sometimes seem cold and withdrawn, though still capable of the gentle gaiety that is evident in her paintings. The advent of grandchildren pleased her greatly. She never lost her gift for balancing the demands made upon her with her need to paint ('You have genius in your life as well as in your art,' Roger Fry once told her, 'and both are rare things'). The combination in her character of restraint with deep feeling caused Virginia Woolf to liken her sister to 'a bowl of golden water which brims but never overflows'.

VANESSA BELL
Duncan Grant, 1917

CLIVE BELL (1881–1964)

Clive Bell was drawn into Bloomsbury while at Cambridge with Thoby Stephen. He came from a wealthy but undistinguished background (his father had made a fortune from coal) and was aptly described by Thoby as a cross between Shelley and a country squire. He had at that time a shock of russet curls but these thinned prematurely, revealing an intellectual's tall forehead. At Cambridge and later in Paris, he became convinced that art and learning were two of the highest achievements: the chief drawback to his attaining either was his immense enjoyment of life.

The sybaritic element in his nature gave Bell a natural sociability. He could not enjoy happiness unless those around him shared his mood, and this made him an excellent host. His appetite for gaiety drew from the novelist David Garnett the observation that Clive Bell was the perfect illustration of James Stuart Mill's utilitarian theory: 'A man cannot become rich without enriching his neighbours.'

When Clive Bell proposed to Vanessa Stephen, she at first refused him, perhaps recognising a temperamental difference that weighed against marriage. But after Thoby Stephen's death in 1906, Vanessa perhaps saw that Clive offered her the possibility of entering a happier, saner world. They had two sons, Julian and Quentin, but after 1911 the marriage dissolved into a lasting, respectful friendship. Bell seemed happier with a mistress, and there were many, though his most lasting relationship was with Mary Hutchinson, the wife of the barrister St John Hutchinson. These liaisons did not distract him from the unchanging assumption that his spiritual home remained within Bloomsbury. Indeed, he remained living at Gordon Square and was a regular visitor to Charleston which, from 1939 onwards, became his permanent home.

A writer on art and literature, Bell is best known for his book *Art*. First published in 1914 and often reprinted, it popularised the notion of 'significant form' as the source of aesthetic emotion in art. He continued to spend many hours each day reading and writing articles and books, including *Civilization* (1928), in which he argues that civilisation is characterised by reason, tolerance, discrimination and humour and is dependent on the existence of a (not necessarily hereditary) leisured élite. Much of his art criticism was indebted to the stimulation of Roger Fry's friendship. He devoted a chapter to Fry in his book of essays, *Old Friends* (1956).

CLIVE BELL, Roger Fry, *c.*1924

In turn, Fry enjoyed Bell's lively mind, but he had reservations about Bell's opinions on modern art and resented the way in which he used his (Fry's) ideas and made them more dogmatic and less flexible.

In Fry's portrait, Bell is seated on a chair made at the Omega Workshops, run by Fry and others between 1913 and 1919, in an attempt to introduce a Post-Impressionist sense of colour and design into the field of applied arts. A set of these chairs can be found in the dining-room at Charleston, where this portrait may have been painted in the mid-1920s, a period during which Fry's interests had returned to the Old Masters.

DUNCAN GRANT
Self-portrait, *c.*1909

DUNCAN GRANT (1885–1978)

When Duncan Grant painted this self-portrait, around 1909, he was still uncertain of the direction that he wanted his art to take. This is one of the most striking of several drawn or painted self-portraits that he produced at this time, yet the manner of painting, in contrast with his searching gaze, suggests uncertainty: it is executed by an artist who is looking for a way forward, in a style shadowed by his knowledge of the Old Masters.

Grant had left school early in order to study at the Westminster School of Art, after which he trained under Jacques-Emile Blanche in Paris. On his return to London in the summer of 1908, he began to pursue friendships that came through his cousins, the Stracheys, and before long he had become part of the Bloomsbury circle. Though not an intellectual and relatively uneducated, he was well read, paradoxically witty and able to hold his own among these intellectuals.

In November 1909 Grant took two rooms on the second floor of 21 Fitzroy Square, becoming a near neighbour of Adrian and Virginia Stephen, who also lived on the west side of the square, eight doors away. 'A close friendship sprang up between Adrian Stephen and myself,' Grant recalled, 'and I had only to tap on the window to be let in. The maid told Virginia "that Mr Grant gets in everywhere". But very irregular as my visits were, they became more and more a habit, and I think they soon became frequent enough to escape notice.'

From then on, Duncan Grant, though an elusive mercurial figure, remained very much at the centre of the Bloomsbury set. He witnessed the excitement caused by Roger Fry's two Post-Impressionist exhibitions in 1910 and 1912 and himself responded immediately to the new ideas about art. Almost overnight he abandoned descriptive skills in favour of more expressive means of representation. His willingness to try a variety of styles and methods made him, for a period, something of an artistic chameleon. He experimented boldly with heightened and in some cases non-naturalistic colour, and often introduced a degree of distortion for rhythmic and witty effects. In the summer of 1911 he painted two scenes, 'Football' and 'Bathing', as part of a scheme to decorate the Borough Polytechnic dining-hall. One critic, unprepared for the lack of patriotic or moralistic sentiment, feared the murals would have a degenerate effect on the students, but most picked out Duncan Grant's work for praise. 'Mr Duncan Grant will one day be heard of beyond the walls of the Borough Polytechnic,' wrote Robert Ross in the *Morning Post*. 'Perhaps he is the Millais of the New Pre-Raphaelites.'

After the First World War, Grant reverted to more traditional methods of representation. He was regarded as one of Britain's leading artists during the inter-war period, and during the course of his highly successful career received many commissions, including decorations for the RMS *Queen Mary*, for Berwick church in Sussex and for Lincoln Cathedral. Although in the 1950s and early 1960s his work was out of fashion, it underwent a revival after Wildenstein's gave him a major retrospective in 1964. His painting, even when it reverts to overly familiar methods of representation, always reveals an alert, interpretative colour sense and an animated sensuousness. There is also a lilting, lyrical quality to his vision, best seen in his landscapes, in his imaginative figure scenes and in his drawings.

Duncan Grant inspired huge affection, partly because he accepted whatever situation he found himself in and always took people on their own terms. His association with Vanessa Bell, which began around 1913 and lasted until her death in 1961, made him an essential ingredient in the life of Charleston. Virginia Woolf, visiting the house in the summer of 1922, noted: 'Charleston is as usual. One hears Clive shouting in the garden before one arrives. Nessa emerges from a great variegated quilt of asters and artichokes; not very cordial; a little absent minded. Then Duncan drifts in, also vague, absent minded, and incredibly wrapped round with yellow waistcoats, spotted ties, and old blue stained painting jackets. His trousers have to be hitched up constantly. He rumples his hair … he requires, I think, peace for painting.'

This peace was largely provided by Vanessa Bell, who had a gift for managing domestic matters. She also gave Duncan Grant a daughter, Angelica. His long and powerful relationship with Vanessa ran alongside his many passions for men. People of both sexes and all ages fell in love with him. A deeply compassionate man, gentle and wholly without self-importance, he brought to any occasion a sense of fun, his quietly festive character irradiating the lives of many. In old age (he lived to be ninety-three) he continued to make young friends.

ROGER FRY (1866–1934)

As a young painter and art critic in the late 1890s and first decades of this century, Roger Fry distrusted much modern art. He looked at the work of his colleagues in the New English Art Club and found it wanting. Rejecting the naturalism of his contemporaries, he turned his attention to the Old Masters whose structural approach Fry admired. Devoting much of his time to writing, he continued to paint in his spare time, his

ROGER FRY, Self-portrait, *c.*1933

ROGER FRY, Ramsey and Muspratt, 1932

pictures recalling those of the seventeenth-century land-scape painter Claude Lorrain in their aspiration towards classical harmony and design.

Much was to happen before Fry shifted his allegiance to modern art. He was busily working as an art critic, for the *Burlington Magazine*, which he helped found, and for the Metropolitan Museum of Art in New York during those years in which 'Bloomsbury' came into existence. Though he was known to various members of this group, he did not join the central core of friends until 1910, when he met Clive and Vanessa Bell by chance at Cambridge railway station. In the course of their journey to London, they talked mostly about modern French art and the need for it to be shown in London. It was no idle talk, as later that year Fry, with Clive Bell's help, mounted the exhibition entitled 'Manet and the Post-Impressionists' at the Grafton Galleries.

Between the meeting at the railway station and the opening of the exhibition, Fry made his first appearance at 46 Gordon Square. Vanessa Bell's sister, Virginia Stephen (later Virginia Woolf), afterwards vividly recalled how he had appeared 'in a large ulster coat, every pocket of which was stuffed with a book, a paint box or something intriguing'. He was older than most of the Bloomsbury set and gave Virginia Woolf the impression that 'he had more knowledge and experience than the rest of us put together'. His passport into her life was probably the way in which he began talking about a recently published French novel and drew everyone present into a discussion of literature.

With hindsight, 1910 can be seen as a pivotal year in Fry's life. He had been shocked to discover, while working as European Advisor to the Metropolitan Museum of Art in New York, that the chairman, the fabulously wealthy J. Pierpont Morgan, had been putting his own interests as a collector before those of the museum he ostensibly served. Fry, who came from a strict Quaker background, made his opinions known and immediately lost his job. At the same time he was faced with an appalling decision concerning his wife, who for some years had hovered on the brink of permanent insanity. Early in 1910, on medical advice, he agreed to have her certified and committed to an asylum. The pain of this decision liberated him from petty precautions and from any desire for prestige or status: now nothing could deflect him from pursuing those interests in which he believed.

In 1910 Roger Fry was prepared to gamble his reputation on a hunch that Van Gogh, Gauguin, Cézanne and other Post-Impressionist painters, though derided and deplored by many British art critics, were artists of importance and worthy of attention. As a result, Fry scandalised precisely those people who had previously sat at his feet when he lectured on Italian Renaissance artists. Nevertheless, he went on to become the impresario of a new movement in art, wrote, lectured and held exhibitions that cumulatively promoted a new aesthetic. Convinced that the new sense of rhythm and colour animating Post-Impressionism should enter and enliven the field of applied arts, Fry founded the Omega Workshops in 1913, which produced all kinds of decorated furniture and objects as well as fabric, rug and carpet designs.

As a painter, though he experimented bravely for a period, Fry later fell back on pre-Post-Impressionist styles. It puzzled his viewers to find that this critic, who had written so passionately about Matisse and Picasso, should himself paint in a style that sometimes looked back to Corot or Chardin or even Claude Lorrain. Towards the end of his life, he painted several self-portraits, including the one in the National Portrait Gallery (c.1933), in which he seems to question the various possibilities of style and expression. These paintings also reinforce the view he held of himself: that, despite all his multifarious activities, he was first and foremost, for better or worse, a painter. After he died, Virginia Woolf wrote in her diary: 'Such a blank wall. Such a silence: such a poverty. How he reverberated.'

LYTTON STRACHEY, Henry Lamb, 1914

LYTTON STRACHEY (1880–1932)

Lytton Strachey was the eleventh child of Sir Richard Strachey, who spent thirty years in India as a soldier and public administrator and then settled with his family at 69 Lancaster Gate, a tall, ugly London house with only one lavatory. After an unhappy and sickly childhood, Lytton Strachey finished his schooling in Liverpool and then went up to Trinity College, Cambridge. Until that time this tall, lanky, invalidish schoolboy had seemed to his cousin Duncan Grant an 'intensely nervous, easily perplexed' character, 'timorous and savage by turns', but Cambridge transformed him. There he encountered a liberal attitude and a mental stimulation that acknowledged intellectual integrity but also licensed his delight in bawdy humour and salacious wit.

Strachey's sensitivity and quick mind gave him a feline receptiveness. At Cambridge he began to invite confidences from others. 'Always there was this atmosphere,' his fellow-student Clive Bell recalled, 'that sense of intelligent understanding mingled with affection.' He became a member of the Apostles, a secret society, but gossiped freely with Duncan Grant about the personalities associated with it. Like others at that time, he fell under the influence of the philosopher G.E. Moore, who stressed the importance of aesthetic emotion and personal relationships.

Increasingly, as Strachey became more self-confident, he displayed a subtly anarchic mind. The pleasure he gave others came not only from his humour and wit but also from his detachment from habitual ways of thinking and behaving: everything he did – even the way he stood, sat or buttered his bread – differentiated him from the crowd.

The lens that Strachey turned on life exposed the preposterous, the sad or absurd in human character, appearance and behaviour. An instance of his ability to see further than most is his description of a doughty Cambridge matron, the philosopher Henry Sidgwick's widow: 'a faded monolith of ugly beauty, with a nervous laugh and an infinitely remote mind, which mysteriously realises all'. To listen to him talk, or to receive his letters, was to share his acute, often slightly hysterical view of the world and to be invited to giggle at it as often as at himself. He hated pretentiousness and any form of cant, rebelling especially against a religion that had been the cause of much sexual oppression.

LYTTON STRACHEY, Simon Bussy, 1904

Strachey's failure to attain an academic career made him a man of letters. He wrote extensively for periodicals, including the *Spectator*, *Nation* and *Athenaeum*, and in 1912 published his first book, *Landmarks in French Literature*. His desire to replace the hagiography that had marred many Victorian biographies with a more ironic approach led to his writing *Eminent Victorians* (1918), with its biographical essays on Cardinal Manning, Florence Nightingale, Thomas Arnold and General Gordon. It was followed by an irreverent but affectionate life of Queen Victoria (1921) and *Elizabeth and Essex: A Tragic History* (1928), which showed, in its interpretation of Essex, a debt to Freud.

Tall and thin, with a long red beard, Strachey attracted the devotion of the painter Dora Carrington, with whom he eventually set up home, first at Tidmarsh Mill, near Pangbourne, and then at Ham Spray in Wiltshire. While at Tidmarsh, Carrington contemplated his routine existence in her diary: 'Outwardly it's like the life of one of the hens. Meals dividing up the day, books read in the morning, siesta, walk to Pangbourne, more books. A French lesson with me, perhaps dinner, reading aloud. Bed and hot water bottles, and everyday the same apparently. But inside, what a variety, and what fantastic doings. And great schemes I suspect.'

It is Henry Lamb's famous portrait of Lytton Strachey (now in the Tate Gallery) that perhaps best catches something of the writer's irony and wit. Strachey's lassitude is successfully captured, echoed in the branches of the trees and mocked by his tightly furled umbrella.

Dora Carrington (1893–1932)

'I often hope I shall die at forty,' Dora Carrington once wrote to the writer Gerald Brenan. 'I could not bear the ignominy of becoming a stout boring elderly lady with a hobby of sketching in watercolours.'

There was little likelihood of this, given the intensity with which Carrington lived. At the age of seventeen, when she entered the Slade School of Art, she threw off her conventional, middle-class upbringing, dropped her first name ('I dislike the Victorian sentimentality of "Dora"') and became Carrington *tout court*. At a time when young women signalled their arrival at adulthood by putting up their hair, she cut hers off, becoming one of the first 'cropheads' (a term coined by Virginia Woolf).

Carrington was even then a strange mixture of naïveté and sophistication. Her bobbed hair, plain dresses and habit of walking with her feet turned in made her look awkward and vulnerable. Yet she also won prizes, became, in the painter Paul Nash's memory, 'a conspicuous and

Lytton Strachey and Dora Carrington
Unknown photographer, 1920s

39

DORA CARRINGTON
Unknown photographer, 1920s

popular figure' and caused Mark Gertler and the Futuristic painter C.R.W. Nevinson to fall in love with her.

She was a student at the time at which Roger Fry's two Post-Impressionist exhibitions had an explosive effect on British art. Though she never became an ardent modernist, her encounter with Post-Impressionism increased her confidence in her own vision. She had an intense feeling for nature, and in certain of her paintings, such as *Farm at Watendlath* (Tate Gallery), she achieved a poetic intensity that aligns her more readily with the Pre-Raphaelites than Post-Impressionism.

Towards the end of her life, Carrington admitted to Gerald Brenan: 'I would like to paint like Uccello and I never shall ... it has something – this desire – to do with my wish to have Lytton [Strachey] as a lover, a wish which the verriest goose could have known was impossible.' Her association with the biographer Lytton Strachey began soon after she left the Slade, in 1915. Invited by Vanessa Bell to spend three days at Asheham,

in Sussex, Carrington was out walking on the South Downs with the rest of the party when Strachey suddenly kissed her. Furious, for she found this lanky intellectual physically repugnant, she decided to take her revenge the next morning and, while he was still asleep, she crept into his bedroom with a pair of scissors. Just as she was about to cut off his long red beard, he opened his eyes and returned her gaze. Immediately her hatred turned to love.

Their compatibility surprised many. Strachey, thirteen years older than Carrington, had a scholar's mind, whereas she was intuitive – an avid reader but relatively uneducated. Though, early in their relationship, they did occasionally share a bed, Strachey remained a practising homosexual. Paradoxically, Carrington's ability to love a man, to adore every detail of his physical person, was unleashed by Strachey, who was, with her, sexually undemanding. There was never any talk of marriage, but they set up home together, first at Tidmarsh Mill in Berkshire, then at Ham Spray, near the Wiltshire Downs.

The couple were visited at Tidmarsh by Rex Partridge, a friend of Carrington's brother. A soldier who had attained the rank of major at twenty-three, he enjoyed argumentative talk and wanted to sail the Mediterranean, trade in wine and dress like a brigand. Carrington invited him to make return visits. 'I say, do you mind if La Majora comes over on Sunday to till our soil?' she asked Lytton. 'He seemed so lonely and bleated so winningly that I gave in. I will keep him on the potato patch, so you won't hardly notice him.' Lytton, however, did notice him, renamed him 'Ralph' and enjoyed long conversations with him. It pleased both when he became part of their household and found a job working for Leonard and Virginia Woolf at the Hogarth Press.

In 1922 Carrington married Partridge, to prevent him going abroad. She knew Strachey had come to rely on his friendship, and she had heard, secondhand, that Strachey dreaded her becoming too dependent, a kind of permanent limpet on his life. The marriage was not a success but the *ménage à trois* continued. Its happiness owed much to Carrington's gift for home-making, and after the move to Ham Spray in 1924, she spent a great deal of her time decorating the house and making it habitable. Yet the cost of her passionate but imperfect relationship with Lytton Strachey told on her. One telling description has been left by his niece, Julia Strachey:

> *From a distance she looked a young creature, innocent and a little awkward, dressed in very odd frocks such as one would see in some quaint old picture-book; but if one came closer and talked to her, one soon saw age scored round her eyes – and something, surely, a bit worse than that – a sort of illness, bodily or mental, which sat oddly on so unspoilt a little face, with its healthy pear-blossom complexion. She had darkly bruised, hollowed, almost battered sockets; and the strange eyes themselves, wide, clear and light as a Northern sky, were not particularly comforting, because of her look of blindness – a statue's blindness screening her own feelings.*

> (Julia: A Portrait of Julia Strachey by herself and Frances Partridge, 1983, p.120)

'He had the power of altering me', Carrington wrote after Lytton Strachey died of stomach cancer on 21 January 1932. But the difference he made had not given her sufficient strength to go on living after his death. After visiting Carrington, Virginia Woolf wrote that she 'seemed helpless, deserted, like some small animal'. The following day, 11 March 1932, alone at Ham Spray, she took hold of a gun she had obtained for shooting rabbits and shot herself in the chest. She was thirty-eight.

LADY OTTOLINE MORRELL (1873–1938)

'Stagnation is what I fear; adventure and failure are far, far better.' Breasting life on these terms, Lady Ottoline Morrell sailed like a Spanish galleon through the dangerous waters of life. She was never part of Bloomsbury but a friend and patron, for she acted as a magnet for artists and writers. She attracted admiration, yet was also mercilessly pilloried. ('Lady Omega Muddle', Lytton Strachey nicknamed her, while in *Private Eye* she became 'Lady Utterly Immoral'.) Given the conflicting views she aroused, it is hard to decide whether she was preposterous or sublime.

LADY OTTOLINE MORRELL, Simon Bussy, *c.*1920

LADY OTTOLINE MORRELL, Augustus John, 1919

An aristocrat, Ottoline Cavendish-Bentinck grew up at Welbeck, with her half-brother, the sixth Duke of Portland. She was strongly aware of her illustrious ancestors: 'As I get old I value this', she wrote, 'and *feel* it subconsciously, secretly as a force.' Nor could she forget that as a child she had played with a dagger that had belonged to Henry VIII and found an ear-ring that Charles I had worn to his execution. It was rumoured that her pearls had belonged to Marie-Antoinette.

Edith Sitwell once remarked that if one is a greyhound one should not try to look like a Pekinese. This Lady Ottoline instinctively knew. She added to her six-foot stature by wearing high heels and enormous hats, becoming, in Osbert Sitwell's eyes, 'an animated public monument'. She dressed in rich brocades and, after the success of the Russian Ballet in London, costumes that displayed a taste for the exotic. Even in old age, disfigured by an operation to her jaw and by then encrusted with face-powder, she still impressed. Story has it that when she dined in restaurants, waiters climbed onto tables to get a better look.

Simon Bussy's portrait (now in the Tate Gallery) emphasises Lady Ottoline Morrell's Habsburg nose and unending chin. She did not seem to mind what artists made of her, and there are also striking portraits by Augustus John and Duncan Grant. She was less happy with the cruel likenesses of her self that appeared in print. She was satirised as 'Lady Rusholme' in Gilbert Cannan's *Pugs and Peacocks*, lampooned as 'Lady Septuagesima Goodley' in Osbert Sitwell's *Triple Fugue*, and recognisably the source for the power-hungry 'Lady Hermione Roddice' in D.H. Lawrence's *Women in Love*. Eleanor Bron's performance as 'Lady Hermione' in Ken Russell's film has helped fix the image of Lady Ottoline in popular imagination.

As Lady Ottoline's biographer Miranda Seymour has remarked, the chief attraction of her husband, Philip Morrell, was that he was too weak a character to dictate the form the marriage should take. He did, however, assist her with the Thursday 'At Homes' that she held at their house in Bedford Square before and during the early part of the First World War. Bloomsbury came to these, talked and danced; they also enjoyed the hospitality that Lady Ottoline offered to many at Garsington Manor in Oxfordshire. Beneath her confusingly theatrical manner lay a genuine desire to nurture the creativity in others, and for that, as well as her appearance, she is remembered.

JOHN MAYNARD KEYNES (1883–1946)

M aynard Keynes was painted by Duncan Grant, Roger Fry and
William Roberts, all of whom caught vivid likenesses. However, it
was Gwen Raverat who, in a watercolour sketch of *c.*1908, best conveyed
Keynes's habit, when listening to another talk, of putting his head on one
side, and with a kind, tolerant smile, seeming to caress the speaker with
his detached, reflective interest. His speculative mind would search out
hidden connections or, with an unexpected frankness, make a sudden
parry and thrust that left his listener surprised by an increase in self-
knowledge. His power over others, chiefly exercised through his eyes,
caused Lytton Strachey to write: 'Keynes sits like a decayed and amorous
spider in King's, weaving purely imaginary webs, noticing everything that
happens and doesn't happen, and writing to me every other post.'

In his fourth year at King's College, Cambridge, Keynes had been
undecided whether his main intellectual preoccupation was economics or
moral philosophy. Opting for the former in 1908, he took up a lecture-
ship at Cambridge and in 1915 joined the Treasury. In 1919, his book *The
Economic Consequences of the Peace* placed him at the centre of a controversy
about the economic reconstruction of Europe, but his most original contribution to the study of economics was his two-volume work *A Treatise on
Money* (1930).

In addition to a mass of books, articles, reviews, academic papers, lec-
tures and essays, he found time also to make and lose several speculative
fortunes, marry the ballerina Lydia Lopokova, form a picture and book
collection and found a theatre, and eventually, to play a leading role in the
creation of the Arts Council of Great Britain.

Keynes's friendship with Lytton Strachey, his affair with Duncan Grant
and his lasting respect for Vanessa Bell, whom he helped with her financial affairs, made him a key figure within Bloomsbury. However, his close
involvement with high finance and politics often wrong-footed him with
his friends, either because he was privy to more information than they or
because a certain worldliness had blunted his sensibility.

In 1920, Virginia Woolf caught sight of Keynes by lamplight and
thought him 'like a gorged seal, double chin, ledge of red lip, little eyes,
sensual, brutal, unimaginative'. Very different is the dark-haired, slim
young man whom Gwen Raverat portrayed. This is the Keynes who

JOHN MAYNARD KEYNES, Gwen Raverat, *c.*1908

looked at the world through amused eyes, his brilliant, sly mind cease-lessly analysing his every encounter with people and ideas. Some years later, Lytton Strachey wrote of Keynes: 'An immensely interesting figure – partly because, with his curious typewriter intellect, he's also so oddly and unexpectedly emotional.'

E.M. FORSTER (1879–1970)

Cambridge University is the connection between the novelist E.M. Forster and the Bloomsbury group. After an unhappy period at Tonbridge School, which left him with a lasting dislike of public-school values and asphyxiating pressures to conform, Forster went up to King's College, Cambridge, which he found much more congenial. Slightly older than Lytton Strachey and Leonard Woolf, he shared with them an admiration for the philosopher G.E. Moore, was elected to the secret society known as 'the Apostles' and became drawn into Bloomsbury, though he was never a central figure. However, his respect for nonconformity, his belief in the sanctity of the individual, his love of rural traditions, of art, the inner life and personal relations all gave him an essential accord with Bloomsbury.

He published his first novel, *Where Angels Fear to Tread*, in 1905, and followed it with a remarkable burst of creativity: *The Longest Journey* appeared in 1907, *A Room with a View* in 1908 and *Howards End* in 1910. However, *A Passage to India*, begun before the First World War, was not published until 1924, and though he pursued a wide range of literary activities, no further novels were published in his lifetime. Inspired by a visit he had paid in 1913 to the home of the visionary Edward Carpenter, who lived openly with a working-class male lover, he wrote a homosexual novel, *Maurice*, which was published posthumously, as was his collection of short stories, *The Life to Come*, many with homosexual themes.

Forster had undistinguished looks, a fluctuating moustache, narrow hands and feet and a confidential voice. He was first painted by Roger Fry in 1911. 'Roger Fry is painting me,' he wrote to a friend. 'It is too like me at present, but he is confident he will be able to alter that. Post-Impressionism is at present confined to my lower lip … and to my chin on which soup has apparently dribbled. For the rest you have a bright, healthy young man, without one hand it is true, and very queer legs, perhaps the result of an aeroplane accident, as he seems to have fallen from an immense height onto a sofa.' Carrington's portrait, painted some years later, is more evocative of his feline nature and subtle irony, owing to its attention to the delicate fall of light.

In 1929 Forster observed in his Commonplace Book that a gulf had widened between himself and Bloomsbury. Nevertheless, he remained a

E.M. FORSTER
Dora Carrington, 1920

EDWARD CARPENTER, Roger Fry, exhibited 1894

member of the Memoir Club (which had been formed in 1920, had no rules, save the understanding that members were free to say anything they pleased) and was present at many Bloomsbury gatherings. When he stayed with his Bloomsbury friends at Charleston and Rodmell, he sometimes found his visits a little chilly and once burned his trousers by standing too close to an electric fire. Virginia Woolf, bumping into Forster at Waterloo Station, likened him to a blue butterfly: 'I mean by that to describe his transparency and lightness.' She concluded: 'I like Forster very much, though I find him whimsical and vagulous to an extent that frightens me with my own clumsiness and definiteness.'

FRANCES PARTRIDGE (born 1900)

Frances Partridge belongs to second-generation Bloomsbury. Though not part of the original core ('Old' Bloomsbury, as Leonard Woolf termed it), she was very close to some of the central figures. She upholds their belief in the importance of friendship and in her diaries, a large portion of which have now been published, maintains many of the attitudes and beliefs associated with Bloomsbury.

She was born Frances Marshall and brought up in Bedford Square in Bloomsbury. From her bedroom window she could watch the horse-drawn buses travelling up and down the Tottenham Court Road. In 1918 she went up to Newnham College, Cambridge. For Part 2 of her tripos she read moral sciences – philosophy, psychology, logic and ethics, subjects that left her, she later realised, 'wanting a realistic attitude to life, with a passion for truth and an interest in the way people's minds work'.

On going down from Cambridge, Frances found a job in the bookshop run by David Garnett and Francis Birrell which was patronised by the Bloomsbury group. She soon caught the attention of Clive Bell, who praised her 'gravely humorous and airily competent mind'. He also put on record that her legs were the prettiest in London.

When Ralph Partridge fell in love with her, it was a development that complicated matters, as he was already married to Dora Carrington. Carrington had agreed to marry Partridge in order to keep near at hand the man on whom Lytton had come to depend. When Partridge took up with Frances Marshall, Strachey, fearing that his ménage was breaking down, arranged to meet her in London. From this pivotal interview emerged the agreement that Ralph and Frances would manage their relationship without damaging the existing state of affairs.

In 1933, the year after Strachey's death and Carrington's suicide, Ralph and Frances married and went to live at Ham Spray. Frances was keen to apply her mind to a literary project and worked with Ralph on an unabridged edition of the Greville memoirs. She also brought up their son, Burgo, and compiled the index for James Strachey's translation of Freud, which runs to twenty-two volumes. After her husband's death in 1960, she moved to Belgravia and in 1978 published *Memories*, the first of several books in which she celebrated many Bloomsbury figures, their descendants and fringe admirers.

FRANCES PARTRIDGE, Derry Moore, 1992

Frances Partridge's published diaries have become touchstones for an attitude of mind that upholds rationalism and intellectual honesty. Despite the suffering caused by the loss of her husband and the tragic early death of her son, she retains a distrust in religious belief and places her faith in what human consciousness can achieve. 'What magnificent sanity,' she wrote in her diary after listening to a Handel fugue. 'In a few bars he convinced me, against all reason, of life being worth living.' On another occasion, after a period in which she had completely lost heart, she found herself on a late autumn day observing the arbitrary groupings of people, dogs and activities in Hyde Park and felt 'a sort of exhilaration – an utterly irrational sense that the stuff of life is good'.

GERALD BRENAN (1894–1987)

Gerald Brenan was descended from three generations of professional soldiers. In 1912, aged eighteen, wanting to escape his father and Sandhurst, he set out with the wandering scholar John Hope-Johnstone, to walk to China. Fearing capture, Brenan fled England disguised as a gas-fitter, complete with butterfly collar, bowler hat and dyed hair.

After several hundred miles, Hope-Johnstone beat a retreat to Venice for the winter. Brenan went on alone until on top of a Bosnian mountain he decided he had reached the end of his resources in every sense. He returned home the prodigal son and agreed to prepare for entrance into the Indian police. In the meantime his reading of Rimbaud, Thoreau's *Walden* and George Borrow only deepened further his desire for self-sufficiency and travel. At this stage he also wanted to become a poet.

The First World War broke into Brenan's dreams. He entered the army and emerged from it in 1919 with the Military Cross. While waiting for action, he had announced, 'I have only one desire – the desire to suffer.'

GERALD BRENAN, John Hope-Johnstone, *c.*1922 (detail)

GERALD BRENAN, Dora Carrington, 1921

If his fascination with pain and deprivation later enhanced his under-standing of Spanish mystics, his real and most continuous desire was simply to read. He sat reading, like an anchorite, for hours in his dug-out. An inability to read he interpreted as a sign of deadness. 'Only a few days ago', he wrote from the trenches, 'it [his desire to read] was alive, and all day I was able to read the gospels and Tolstoy with eagerness … Worst sign – I have ceased to be able to read poetry.'

While in the army, Brenan began a lifelong friendship with Ralph Par-tridge, who was in love with, and eventually married Dora Carrington. Unfortunately for Brenan, he fell in love with Carrington while visiting

Partridge, wooed her for three years and slept with her only once. Despite the agony it caused him, he later claimed to V.S. Pritchett: 'I was as proud of my affair with her as I was of having been in the line at Passchendaele. The tears I shed for her were, I thought, my true medals.'

In 1920, with financial help from a great aunt, Brenan went to live in a remote region of Spain; he took with him 2,000 books. He liked the emptiness of Spain and its bone-coloured rocks and hills. 'In such a country one can breathe', he said. After walking some 630 miles, he found Yegen, which is 4,000 feet above sea-level. It gave him 'the feeling of fields of air washing over one', and he told his brother: 'This is my desert island.'

Yegen was then one of the poorest villages in the Alpujarra, and in time Brenan came to see Spain's vast agrarian problems as the greatest single cause of the Spanish Civil War. From the start, he experienced a natural kindliness from the natives, finding, as George Orwell said, that Spaniards have 'a generosity, a species of nobility that do not usually belong to the twentieth century'. Eventually he used the notes he made on Yegen in his *South from Granada*, the first of several books that made him renowned as a writer on Spanish people, history and literature.

Partridge, Carrington and Lytton Strachey all set out to visit Brenan in Spain in 1921. In order to reach Yegen, they ended their journey on mules, crossing and recrossing a river that led up a mountainside. Strachey, suffering from piles, was in agony. When three years later he learnt that Leonard and Virginia Woolf were likewise preparing to visit Brenan, he warned, 'It's *Death! Death!*'

In 1992 his biographer, Jonathan Gathorne-Hardy, revealed that Brenan's marriage to the poet and novelist Gamel Woolsey was bigamous: in order to annul Gamel's first marriage, a trip to New York would have been necessary, and this, Brenan judged, was too expensive. He was none too faithful to Gamel, and seven weeks after she died, Lynda Price, a girl of twenty-four, moved in: the next sixteen years were some of the happiest in Brenan's life. When he reached the age of ninety-one, he was sent back to Britain and put in an old people's home in Pinner. Some Andalusians, not wishing him to endure such indignity, kidnapped him and returned him – by then a piece of Spanish national treasure – to the country in which he belonged and where, in 1987, he died.

DAVID GARNETT (1892–1981)

The young David Garnett began to appear at Bloomsbury parties shortly before the First World War. He was then studying botany at the Royal College of Science and had become a regular at Adrian Stephen's poker parties. Through these he met Duncan Grant, who fell in love with him.

Between 1915 and 1919 Grant and Garnett lived together in a *ménage à trois* that involved Vanessa Bell. During that time she had a child by Grant, a daughter whom she named Angelica. Garnett, watching the baby being weighed in a shoe-box on some kitchen scales, conceived the idea of marrying her. More than twenty years later he did so, and it was one of their four daughters, Nerissa Garnett, who painted this vibrant portrait.

Though too young to have been part of 'Old' Bloomsbury, Garnett came from an extremely bookish background. Both his grandfather and his great grandfather had occupied key positions in the British Museum's Reading Room, his grandfather, Richard Garnett, becoming the chief editor of the library's first printed catalogue. His father, Edward Garnett, doyen of publishers' readers, had been of crucial help to D.H. Lawrence, Joseph Conrad and others, and his mother, Constance Garnett, was a distinguished translator, responsible for introducing many Russian classics to British readers.

David Garnett turned to literature whilst running a bookshop in Soho. His early success with *Lady into Fox* (1922), an enigmatic fable about a young wife who is transformed into a fox, was modelled on Defoe. It began his fertile career as a novelist, though none of his subsequent books enjoyed the success of his first. His three-volume autobiography has made an important contribution to the history of the Bloomsbury group, and he also edited the letters of T.E. Lawrence, the novels of Thomas Love Peacock and his own correspondence with T.H. White.

Garnett first married Frances Partridge's sister Ray Marshall, with whom he moved to Hilton Hall, near Cambridge. They had two sons and for some fifteen years Garnett remained a little apart from his Bloomsbury friends. After Ray's death from cancer in 1940, he married Angelica Bell, and though this exposed complicated feelings in his relations with Duncan Grant and Vanessa Bell, it gradually drew him back into the Bloomsbury circle.

DAVID GARNETT
Nerissa Garnett, *c.*1970

With his cornflower-blue eyes, his slow tempo and staunch affection for his friends, David Garnett was much loved by others. Confident of his own opinions, he enjoyed many friendships with artists and writers, some of whom he celebrated in his collection of essays, *Great Friends* (1979).

PHILIPPA STRACHEY (1872–1968) AND
MARJORIE STRACHEY (1882–1964)

❦

Philippa (Pippa) and Marjorie Strachey were sisters of Lytton Strachey, members of the bookish, articulate family that inhabited 69 Lancaster Gate. Over it presided their mother, Lady Strachey, always ready to take part in a play-reading, to enter a literary or political discussion, adept at billiards and an old hand at teaching young people how to dance a Highland reel; it was impossible to be bored in her presence.

Ever since reading John Stuart Mill's essay *On Liberty*, Lady Strachey had been a feminist. She had helped circulate the first petition to Parliament for women's votes and was a stalwart member of the National Union of Woman's Suffrage Societies (NUWSS), marching regularly in

PHILLIPA STRACHEY
Unknown photographer

LYTTON STRACHEY AND MARJORIE STRACHEY
Unknown photographer, c.1928

their processions, writing pamphlets and fund-raising. Her daughter Pippa shared her beliefs and devoted much of her life to the cause. She became the Secretary of the London and National Society for Women's Service (later the Fawcett Society).

Pippa Strachey was lively, intelligent, sweet-tempered, with a keen sense of the ridiculous and a screeching laugh. When Duncan Grant lodged with the Stracheys as an art student, he found a particular friend in Pippa. It was said of her that she had only to walk on to a railway platform for an engine-driver to lean out of his cabin and unburden himself of his life story.

Marjorie Strachey, the youngest daughter, tried her hand at teaching and at one point ran a school for one term at Charleston. She also wrote, not very successfully, a life of Chopin, *The Song of the Nightingale*. Her most memorable achievement was perhaps her ability to recite nursery rhymes with such exaggerated or unexpected emphasis that the most innocent tale became blood-curdling or full of sexual innuendo.

MARGERY FRY (1874–1958)

Margery Fry could never be called a member of Bloomsbury, but it was she who asked Virginia Woolf to write the biography of her brother, Roger Fry. As Margery was a woman of strong character, with her own opinions as to how the book should be written, there was a good deal of friction between Margery and Virginia Woolf and between her and Bloomsbury in general.

Margery Fry had grown up under the watchful eyes of high-minded Quaker parents. She had five sisters, none of whom ever married, a fact that Margery blamed on their convent-like upbringing: among other restraints, they were forbidden ever to laugh at a joke made by a man, lest they be thought fast. But the narrowness of their upbringing did not prevent these sisters from becoming forceful, independent and notable figures. Margery Fry devoted much of her life to the Howard League for Penal Reform. She was one of the last persons to speak with Ruth Ellis, the last woman to be hanged, and was a deeply committed opponent of capital punishment. She also had a considerable reputation in educational circles, becoming principal of Somerville College, Oxford, and a governor of the BBC.

Especially close to her brother Roger, Margery Fry shared a house with him for a period after the First World War in Dalmeny Avenue, London. In 1932 she accompanied him and Leonard and Virginia Woolf on a holiday to Greece; Virginia Woolf wrote of them to Vanessa Bell:

They [Roger and Margery] hum and buzz like two boiling pots. I've never heard people, after the age of 6, talk so incessantly. What's more, there's not a word of it what you or I might call foolish: it's all about facts and information and at the most trying moments when Roger's insides are falling down [he was suffering from haemorrhages], and Margery must make water instantly or perish, one has only to mention Themistocles and the battle of Plates for them both to become like youth at its spring. The amount they know about art, history, archaeology, biology, stones, sticks, birds, flowers is in fact a constant reproof to me. Margery caught me smiling the other day at my own thoughts and said no Fry has ever done that. "No" said Roger, "we have no power of dissociation," which is why of course they're such bad painters – they never simmer for a second.

(Nigel Nicolson and and J.T. Banks (eds.), The Sickle Side of the Moon: The Letters of Virginia Woolf, Vol. V: 1932–1935, 1979, p.56)

MARGERY FRY, Claude Rogers, 1939

The painter Howard Hodgkin, a distant relation of the Fry family, used to visit Margery Fry as a young man. By then she had retired from Oxford and was living in London, surrounded by her brother's pictures, some of his Old Master paintings and objects made at the Omega Workshops. Hodgkin recalled: 'She had her hair cut short, as was fashionable at the time, in two – they looked a bit like bunches of broccoli – so that they stuck out either side of her head – not flattering. She had the most beautiful eyes and, by the time I knew her, no shape at all: she was just a big bag of beautiful silk.'

Claude Rogers, who painted her portrait in 1939, had founded the Euston Road School of Painting in 1937. Margery Fry did much to support this venture, having to some extent taken up her brother's mantle after his death in 1934. It may have been in appreciation of this that Rogers painted this portrait, its sober mood reflecting the sitter's depth of purpose.

BERTRAND RUSSELL (1872–1970)

There were many points of contact between Bertrand Russell and Bloomsbury, though he was never part of that circle of friends. Like his near contemporaries at Cambridge, Leonard Woolf, Desmond MacCarthy and Lytton Strachey, he delighted in G.E. Moore's clear thinking. 'We all felt electrified by him', Russell recalled, adding that until then they had not known 'what fearless intellect pure and unadulterated really means'. But if, like Strachey, he thought that the Age of Reason dated from the appearance of Moore's *Principia Ethica*, he differed with Strachey on another matter: homosexuality he regarded with contempt.

Once when asked what he had been doing all morning in the company of his former pupil Wittgenstein, Russell replied that they had been discussing whether there were two things in the world or three. Small wonder, therefore, that when Roger Fry painted Russell's portrait he abjured the aesthetically pleasing in favour of a harsh, clear statement of facts. This is the man who once said that mathematics, 'rightly viewed, possess not only truth, but supreme beauty … cold and austere – sublimely pure'. Not surprisingly, this mathematician–philosopher sometimes found human relations intractable and messy. He caused much unhappiness, to his children as well as to cast-off wives and lovers. Not until he was eighty did he appear to settle and find peace. 'I have lived a great deal,' he announced, 'but I am not sated yet.'

Though Russell made his name with *The Principles of Mathematics*, which even today mathematicians find abstruse, he also did important work in the field of logic. In mid-career he allowed his philosophical concerns to broaden, partly in response to financial pressures and the need to reach a wider readership. He wrote on marriage, morals, mysticism, political ideals and the impact of science on society, among other topics, and also became a leading figure in the Campaign for Nuclear Disarmament.

Russell may have wished to avoid contact with Bloomsbury, despite his early friendship with Roger Fry, but his marriage to Logan Pearsall Smith's sister, Alys, entangled him in a social network that overlapped with Bloomsbury at various points. Alys's nieces, Ray and Karin Costelloe, married respectively a Strachey and a Stephen. Moreover Russell's affair with Lady Ottoline Morrell brought him perilously close to centre stage in the theatre of gossip. When she expressed the fear that she was not clever

BERTRAND RUSSELL, Roger Fry, *c*.1923

enough for him, he told her not to worry as 'no woman's intellect is really good enough to give me pleasure as intellect.' His mental journeying continued all his life. In his ninety-sixth year he remarked 'When the time comes to die, I shall have to inform Death that I am too busy just now.'